THE WORD AMONG US

THE HOLY FAMILY
A sculpture in iron
by Joseph Ammann

THE WORD
AMONG US

CHESTER A. PENNINGTON

A PILGRIM PRESS BOOK   *from United Church Press, Philadelphia*

The acknowledgments for previously published material
are listed on page 9.

The biblical quotations are from the *Revised Standard
Version of the Bible,* copyright 1946 and 1952 by the Divi-
sion of Christian Education, National Council of Churches,
and are used by permission. The following passages have
been quoted:
 "A Glad Integrity"—Matt. 5:3-14
 "Better than Good"—Matt. 5:20-22, 27-28, 33-34, 38-39,
  43-44, 48
 "Unpretending Piety"—Matt. 6:1, 3, 5, 16-17
 "A Sense of Value"—Matt. 6:19-25, 32-33
 "Standards of Excellence"—Matt. 7:1, 6-7, 13, 15-16, 21
 "A Prayer to Live By"—Matt. 6:9-13 (13b, KJV)

Library of Congress Cataloging in Publication Data

Pennington, Chester A
 The Word among us.

 "A Pilgrim Press book."
 Poems.
 1. Sermon on the Mount—Meditations. 2. Lord's
prayer—Meditations. I. Title.
BT380.2.P36   242   73-8503
ISBN 0-8298-0259-2

United Church Press, 1505 Race Street,
Philadelphia, Pennsylvania 19102

CONTENTS

ACKNOWLEDGMENTS

Grateful acknowledgment is made to the following publishers to reprint material as follows:

A Contemporary Psalm Text by Chester A. Pennington. Composer: Paul Fetler. A cantata commissioned by the Hennepin Avenue United Methodist Church of Minneapolis, Minnesota, 1968. Reprinted by permission of Augsburg Publishing House, Minneapolis, Minnesota, copyright owner (1969).

The Embodied Word Text by Chester A. Pennington. Composer: Walter Pelz. A cantata commissioned by the Hennepin Avenue United Methodist Church of Minneapolis, Minnesota, 1972. Reprinted by permission of Augsburg Publishing House, Minneapolis, Minnesota, copyright owner (1973).

"Emmanuel" and "The World Knew Him Not," from *With Good Reason* by Chester A. Pennington. Copyright © 1967 by Abingdon Press.

"The Holy Family" pictured on page 4 is from the collection of Chester and Marjorie Pennington.

THE WORD AMONG US

I

Incarnate Word

EMMANUEL: GOD WITH US

He came to us, as if to say,
  I am always with you.
He gave himself, as if to say,
  I am always for you.

But disguised, unknown—
  He was seen
  He was received
Only by those who willed it so.

As then, so now, he is among us
  Disguised, unknown.
His presence waits on our seeing.
His giving waits on our receiving.

Lord, with the gift of thyself,
Grant us grace
  To know thee
  To receive thee
Emmanuel, God with us.

THE WORLD KNEW HIM NOT

Do we yet know him?
　"He was in the world,
　and the world was made through him,
　yet the world knew him not."
How sad, we say, how bad. If we had been there . . .

But
　Like guests at the inn, playing holiday,
　Like soldiers and civil servants, keeping order,
　Like scribes and pharisees, supporting religion,
We may not know him.

Or
　Like shepherds, believing without certainty,
　Like wise men, giving treasure to hope,
　Like father and mother, all tenderness and wonder,
We may know him.

　For he is given to be received,
　He is disclosed to be discovered,
　He is surrendered to be obeyed.

Dear God,
May we truly know him whom thou hast sent.

MARY KEPT ALL THESE
THINGS IN HER HEART

(Thoughts on the Flight into Egypt*)

Mother of God!
Must you still flee the wrath of men,
Shielding your child from the cold of our indifference?

The old priest said,
A sword would pierce your soul as well.
   Is it this you secretly clutch
     With only Joseph to suspect your pain?
And do you sense above you the winged care
Of the tireless love of God?

Keep this in your heart as well:
   He whom you bear is for the healing of the nations,
   Though it be with his stripes that we are healed.

Take quietly then the sword into your heart—
   You will bear with him his pain.
You cannot shield him from the steely wrath of men—
   He will draw this into his own wounds.
And we who are healed, as we sing his name,
   Will rise to call you blest as well.

---

*A wood block print by Sadao Watanabe, contemporary Japanese artist

THE HOLY FAMILY

Some say
The family is breaking up
And may one day prove
No longer relevant in our world.

A person of faith might say:

As long as God is love
He will need these profound relations
Through which to communicate himself.

As long as humans need love
We will require these deep intimacies
In which to discover ourselves.

That as God became man
In the embrace of family,
So we become truly human
In family encounter.

How else
Shall we learn to say, "Our Father..."
Or call to one another, "Brother, Sister."

THE EMBODIED WORD

(An Unfinished Reflection on the Incarnation)

i

In the beginning was the Word,
And the Word was with God,
And the Word was God.
He was in the beginning with God;
  All things were made through him,
    And without him was not anything made that was
      made.[1]

In the beginning of God's creative activity
  There was only chaos.
All was disordered nothingness
  Without form and void.[2]

  Into this darkness, God uttered his Word.
  God said, *"Let there be . . ."*
  And existence comes into being.

Upon all that emerges from nonbeing into becoming
God impresses the order of his own being.
  Chaos takes the form of Cosmos,
  Disorder is shaped into Order,
  Dissonance is resolved into Harmony,
All that exists reflects the reality of the One-Who-Is,
  Who says of himself, "I AM."[3]

---

[1] John 1:1-3
[2] Genesis 1:2
[3] "I AM WHO I AM," Exodus 3:14

Only the sounding of the Word evokes being.
Beyond the reach of the Word there is only nonbeing.
Let the Word cease to sound and existence ceases to be.
All that is exists solely by the creative expression of the
Word.

This is the first embodiment of the Word.

ii

What is thus made
Reflects the order and harmony of God's being,
And is able thus to sustain
A still deeper expression of the personal being of God.

And God said,
"Let us make man in our image." [4]
And man is . . .
Receiving our being from the only One-Who-Really-Is,
Owing our life to the life-giving Word,
So that we exist only in response
To the continuous sounding of the Word.

This is the second embodiment of the Word.
God created man in his own image,
In the image of God he created him;
Male and female he created them. [5]

Our creative urge is our response to the divine creativity.
When we create we imitate—
We may even participate with—
The one whose creative power constitutes all of existence.

---

[4] Genesis 1:26
[5] Genesis 1:27

We find shapes in stones and carve them into forms,
We see lines in colors and give contour to our vision,
We hear sounds, find reeds, strings, skins,
    And tune them to our inner hearing.

Wherever there is beauty
There is the creative bodying forth
Of the divinely implanted Word.

iii

Bearing the heady freedom
    Of giving shape to our own images,
We are tempted to worship our works
    As if we ourselves were divine.

And we create . . .
    A tower of babel, hurling ourselves into chaos,
    A golden calf, plunging hilariously into idolatry,
    A religion, in which darkness is worshiped as light,
    A society, in which brothers slay one another in mind-
        less fear.

There come times when we seem able to speak
    Only in distortion and dissonance,
Giving shape in jagged fragments
    To the broken image of our creator.

    Still the Word seeks to find utterance:
        The Prophet shouts in pain and anger,
        The Priest enacts in reverence and awe,
        The Poet sings in anguish and rapture,
    But the Word is not heard.

The Word must be bodied forth yet more fully.
What had been well done is threatened by our undoing.
  The divine order is shaken by our disarray,
  The cosmic harmony is distorted by our discord.
The creative Word which called all into being
Must be uttered in the call to renewed being.

  And God said, "Let it be . . ."
  And Jesus the Christ is.

  The Word became flesh and dwelt among us,
  Full of grace and truth.[6]

The Word which is implicit in all creation,
  The Word which inheres in our humanity,
The eternal, divine Word becomes truly human.

This is the crucial embodiment of the Word:
  A baby in a bed of straw,
  A boy learning his father's trade,
  A teacher pleading with unhearing listeners,
  A victim writhing on a cross,
  A man emerging mysteriously out of death into life.

---

[6] John 1:14

V

The Eternal submits to the limits of time
    To release us from bondage to our past
    And free us for our future.

The Divine empties himself into the human
    So we may know who we really are
    And become who we are intended to be.

The Creator wills to be the Savior.
    We see love as a man stretched on a cross,
    We know life as a victory won over death.

    To all who received him,
    Who believed in his name,
    He gave power to become children of God.[7]

This event is the moment of truth for all time.
    This life the image of true humanity.
These words the parables by which men shall live.
    This person the saving man for all men everywhere.

    For this I was born, he said,
    And for this I have come into the world.[8]
That meaning may be restored to our life,
That beauty may be wrested from ugliness,
That harmony may give peace to our mind,
That order may make room for justice,
That we may become our own embodiment of the Word.

---

[7] John 1:12
[8] John 18:37

II

Living Words

A GLAD INTEGRITY

*Blessed are
the poor in spirit,
for theirs is
the kingdom
of heaven.*

You are fortunate, indeed,
If you realize that you are not self-sufficient,
If you have learned to rely upon God.

For when you know this,
You no longer have to be defensive—
As if proving how great you are.

You know better;
You are limited, dependent upon God.

And this is your good fortune,
For in this knowledge
You are indeed ruled and directed by him.

Blessed are those
who mourn,
for they shall
be comforted.

Be glad
To be sensitive to suffering.

Life is a joy,
And we celebrate its beauties.
But life is full of suffering,
Its beauties frequently shadowed by sadness.

You will find joy
In accepting your own suffering,
And being sensitive to the hurt of others.

The comfort you gain,
Given by others,
Comes from God,
Who shares in your suffering.

*Blessed are
the meek,
for they
shall inherit
the earth.*

It is good to be gentle.
Gentleness is not a sign of weakness,
But of strength.

It may appear otherwise;
Society may misread the signs.

The self-assertive,
The wielders of power
May seem to get what they want.

But bluff and bluster
Frequently mask a haunting fear.
And the thrust of power
May be the frightened move of the insecure.

Only the strong can be gentle.
And though society seems to bypass them,
Only the gentle receive
What God wants them to have.

Blessed are those
who hunger
and thirst
for righteousness,
for they shall
be satisfied.

You will be satisfied
As you strive for genuine integrity.

If you long for other values,
The goals that are popular in society,
You will be shut up in frustration.

But when you deeply desire
To achieve the integrity which God wills,
You will find true satisfaction.

*Blessed are
the merciful,
for they shall
obtain mercy.*

You are to be congratulated
That you really care for others.

If you care
For those who silently cry out for kindness,
You will receive love.

For kindness is the very character of God.
And in expressing compassion,
You open yourself to the divine mercy.

*Blessed are
the pure in heart,
for they shall
see God.*

You will be happy,
If you are real.

Masks are for games, not for living.
Pretending to be
Somebody you know you are not
Prevents your becoming who you should be.

In becoming a real person,
You will experience the reality of God.
For God is not discovered by argument or logic.
He is discerned by those who are themselves real.

*Blessed are
the peacemakers,
for they shall
be called
sons of God.*

There is joy in reconciling
Those who are at odds with one another.

Breaking down barriers,
Healing differences,
Is doing God's work in the world.
For he wills to reconcile persons to one another.

In serving God as peacemakers,
You are doing his work
As trusted and obedient children.

Blessed are those
who are persecuted
for righteousness' sake,
for theirs is
the kingdom of heaven.

Blessed are you
when men revile you
and persecute you
and utter all kinds of evil
against you falsely
on my account.
Rejoice and be glad,
for your reward is
great in heaven,
for so men persecuted
the prophets
who were before you.

You may even consider yourself fortunate
If you get into trouble
Because of your faithfulness to God.

Obedience to his will,
Faithfulness to his purposes,
May often bring you into conflict with society.

Human defensiveness being what it is,
You are sure to be misunderstood.
Human arrogance being what it is,
You are sure to be opposed.
Indeed,
Human limitations being what they are,
You will never be quite so effective
As you would hope to be—
Or even as you think you are.

So if you run into trouble,
Not just because of your limitations
Or perhaps even your wrongheadedness,
Cheer up—
That's the way it has always been.

Don't avoid trouble,
But don't look for it either.
You are not called to please people
Or to irritate them,
Only to be faithful to God.

You are
the salt
of the earth.

What you are to be
You are to be in the world.

Like salt.

Society has a tendency to go bad.
It needs a preservative,
Men and women committed to human values.

It doesn't take a lot of salt
To do the job—
But you must keep your zest.

Be like salt,
Present in every good thing
Going on in the world.

You are
the light
of the world.

Like light.

People like to see things
As not quite black and white
But an indistinguishable gray.

In this grayness
You are to be like light,
Bringing clarity, aiding vision,
Showing the way.

God is light,
And you are his reflectors.
Perhaps those who see you
Will be turned to him.

BETTER THAN GOOD

I tell you,
unless your
righteousness
exceeds that of
the scribes and Pharisees,
you will never enter
the kingdom
of heaven.

I want you to be
Better than the most religious people
You know or can imagine.

There are laws and customs
Which are essential to society.
But they have nothing to do
With what I am talking about.
I am concerned with the core of your being,
The quality of person that you are.

*You have heard
that it was said
to the men of old,
"You shall not kill..."
But I say to you
that every one
who is angry
with his brother
shall be liable
to judgment.*

There is a law against murder.
Society requires such a law.

But I want you to be
A person purged of anger,
Incapable of an irrational,
Hostile outburst against another person.

*You have heard
that it was said,
"You shall not
commit adultery."
But I say to you
that every one
who looks at a woman
lustfully
has already committed
adultery with her
in his heart.*

The law prohibits adultery.
The stability of marriage and home requires this.

But I want you to be
A person cleansed of the lunging desire
To use another person's body
For your own gratification.

Custom allows divorce
Under certain well-considered circumstances.
Human frailties being what they are,
Society properly allows this.

But I want you to be
A person who values so highly
The union of husband and wife,
That you will enter it
Only with the deepest commitment to one another,
And will do your utmost to cherish its fidelity.

Again you have heard
that it was said
to the men of old,
"You shall not
swear falsely..."
But I say to you,
Do not swear
at all.

The system of justice requires
The taking of oaths.
People can't be trusted to tell the truth
And must be persuaded with threats.

But I want you to be
A person of transparent honesty,
Incapable of deceit,
Whose word is utterly dependable.

You have heard
that it was said,
"An eye for an eye and
a tooth for a tooth."
But I say to you,
Do not resist
one who is evil.

There is a rough-handed justice
Commonly accepted in society.

But I want you to be
A person who will not retaliate at all.
Just don't strike back.
Be open to the one who would exploit you.

You have heard
that it was said,
"You shall love
your neighbor
and hate
your enemy."
But I say to you,
Love your enemies...

You, therefore,
must be perfect,
as your heavenly Father
is perfect.

The usual practice
Is to be decent to those who are decent to you,
And cool—if not hostile—
To those who are indifferent or antagonistic.

I want you to be
A person who meets everyone
With honest goodwill—
Even your opponent.

If you are kind to those who are congenial,
What's so great about that?
Anyone can do this.

I want you
To meet the hateful with kindness,
To meet the arrogant with gentleness,
To meet the hostile with concern.

If you ask me why, the answer is simple:
That's the way God is.

When you were hostile to him,
He met you with unwearied love.
When you were militant against him,
He met you with patient gentleness.
And you are to reflect his character.

In a word,
I want you to be as good as God!

UNPRETENDING PIETY

*Beware of
practicing your piety
before men
in order to be seen
by them.*

Whatever religious practices you follow,
Be sure you do them for the right reason.

Don't do things just to be noticed,
Or because they are expected of you.
Do them because you believe
They are what God wants you to do.

Attitudes and actions have consequences.

If your actions are a mere pretense,
You may be noticed, even admired,
But you will destroy your own integrity.

If you act honestly,
It will not matter whether you are noticed.
You will become a real person.

When you give alms,
do not let
your left hand
know what
your right hand
is doing.

When you engage in acts of benevolence
Don't call attention to what you are doing,
Don't do them just to keep up with your peers.

For then you are not really being benevolent.
You are only doing what others expect of you,
Or what you think will impress them.
And the only satisfaction you will receive
Is that you have conformed,
You have been noticed.

When you act with integrity
You have the satisfaction of knowing
You have done what your humanity requires of you.

And when you pray,
you must not
be like
the hypocrites.

When you go to church,
Don't go just to be noticed.
For you may be noticed
But that's all that will happen.

When you worship,
Do so with honesty,
And God will meet you in your praying.

And when you fast,
do not look dismal...
But when you fast,
anoint your head
and wash
your face.

When you are willing to deny yourself,
Don't call attention to your self-sacrifice.
Don't comment about how much you are giving up.
Do not spoil your religion
By putting on a long face.

Enjoy your faith.
If it requires sacrifice,
Do it gladly.
If the disciplines are sometimes stern,
Engage in them gracefully.

The good life should look good.

A SENSE OF VALUE

Do not lay up
for yourselves
treasures on earth...
But lay up
for yourselves
treasures in heaven....

For where
your treasure is,
there will
your heart be also.

What you value most
Will become the focus of your energies.
The emotional powers of your life
Will circle around whatever compelling motive
Dominates your will.

Therefore, do not be seduced
By the secondary values of your society.
Do not be dominated by the goods
Sought after by your culture.
Rather center your desires
On the values which God endorses.

If your eye is sound,
your whole body
will be full
of light;
but if your eye
is not sound,
your whole body
will be full
of darkness.

If your vision of reality is blurred,
The meaning of your life will be unclear.
If you do not see what is true,
You cannot live truly.
If your vision is such
That darkness appears to be light,
You will forever grope in darkness,
Wondering why you cannot see.

No one can serve
two masters...
You cannot serve
God
and mammon.

You cannot divide your loyalty
Between two values,
For you will surely subordinate one to the other.
Only one mastering desire
Can direct your life.

Do not be anxious
about your life,
what you shall eat
or what
you shall drink,
nor about your body,
what you shall put on.

For
the Gentiles seek
all these things;
and your heavenly Father
knows that you
need them all.

Do not let yourself become anxious
About matters pertaining to your earthly life.
Basic needs become complex obsessions
When they dominate you.
So don't be driven by desire
For measurable achievements.

Obsessive concern with creature comforts
Is paganism—
The worship of this present life
As if it were all that matters.

You must learn to trust God.
Believe that he cares about you,
Your physical well-being
As well as what you call spiritual.

Seek first
his kingdom
and his righteousness,
and all these things
shall be yours
as well.

Let the dominant purpose of your life be
To be ruled by God,
And you may be assured
That secondary values will also be realized.

Persist in your determination
To let God direct your life,
And every human value will be yours.

STANDARDS OF EXCELLENCE

Judge not,
that you be not
judged.

You must learn to make distinctions,
To judge among values.
But do not be quick to condemn others.
Do not reject those who disagree with you.

It is easy to be patient with your own faults,
And impatiently critical of others.
It would be better
To be sensitive to your shortcomings,
And therefore more understanding of others.

You must not judge others
On the basis of external appearances.
You don't know what's going on inside them—
Where the real reasons for behavior are hidden.

Give others the same kindness and consideration
That you would hope to receive.

Do not give dogs
what is holy;
and do not throw
your pearls
before swine,
lest they
trample them under foot
and turn
to attack you.

On the other hand,
You must learn to make evaluations.
To choose among rival appeals,
You need standards of taste and judgment.

In a society threatened by mediocrity,
You must be committed to excellence.

*Ask, and
it will be given you;
seek and
you will find;
knock, and
it will be opened
to you.*

Persist in your faithfulness
Because you trust the goodness of God.
Continue to ask
Because you know God wants to give.
Continue to seek
Because you know God wants to disclose.
Continue to knock
Because you know God wants to respond.

*Enter by
the narrow gate.*

There is an easygoing, likable manner
That is both attractive and popular,
But it leads to self-destruction.

The way to life is difficult and demanding.
Not many are willing to pay the price.
You must be ready to join the minority.

*Beware of
false prophets ...
you will know them
by their fruits.*

There are false prophets
Who make an attractive appeal,
But will destroy your real values.

You will know the true prophets.
Everything they do reflects
Their honest caring for your good.

Not every one
who says to me,
"Lord, Lord,"
shall enter
the kingdom of heaven,
but he who
does the will
of my Father
who is in heaven.

Not everyone will enter the kingdom of God.
You may speak the right words
And do the right things—
But never accept God's rule.

Be the kind of person
Who is open to the will of God.

Build your life on these words.
Such a life will stand the tests of time
And will endure through eternity.

A PRAYER TO LIVE BY

Pray then
like this:
Our Father
who art in heaven

As children learn to trust
Those who give them love,
So you may trust the one who gives you
Not only your being,
But the power of his love.

It is not easy for you to believe:
Your world seems so big;
Your skills increase so quickly;
Your feelings are so confused.

I simply ask your trust.
If you believe in me,
Believe also in God.

This is what I have tried to be for you:
If you have really seen me,
You have seen the Father.

Hallowed be
thy name.

The one whom you trust
Deserves your reverence.

Though I called him "Daddy,"
I never presumed on his goodness.
I always knew who he is.

You must indeed discover and affirm
Your own being.
But you must also know
Yourself sustained
By the only one who is truly good.
So give him honor, praise.

If you saw any wholeness in me,
Know that it was the holiness of our Father,
Accepted and affirmed in myself.

Thy kingdom come

Let your life be ruled by God.
Affirm his purpose as your final goal,
Unrivaled by the largest aims of earth.
Desire his will as a pearl of great price,
A value beyond measure.
Enter his way with the joy of discovery,
As if stumbling on an unexpected find.

Thy will
be done,
On earth
as it is
in heaven.

Open yourself to the possibilities
Of his will for you.

And how may I know, you ask?
You dare to trust he wills
Only your good.

Do not be anxious.
Let his kingdom come
In your attitude of obedience.
Let his will be done
In your openness to his purpose.

As in heaven?

You will be torn
As heavenly creatures are not.
But you may grow into a like faithfulness,
To will one thing:
His purpose
In your place
On earth.

Give us this day
our daily bread

If you are really given to his will,
You may trust him to take care of you.

The trouble is
You want too much.
You try too hard
And don't care deeply about others.

Why not trust him
To allow you what you really need.
Let your faith extend this far:
Your hairs are numbered,
He notes the sparrow,
He cares for you.

And help it come true
That your fellow humans
May have what they need as well.
Use your good gifts
To increase their good.

*And forgive us
our debts,
As we also
have forgiven
our debtors*

As your body needs bread
Your soul needs forgiveness,
Pardon for what you have owed
And have not been able to give,
Obedience to your Father.

Know this as your deepest need,
The gift he most wants to give:
Your self-raised barriers removed,
Oneness with him restored,
The flow of his grace renewed.

Then you will be free to forgive.
As you are fully forgiven,
You are to be truly forgiving.
Seventy times seven.
Freely. Gladly.

*And lead us
not into temptation,
But deliver us
from evil.*

You will live in the constant tension
Between the demand of God
And your own inclining,
Between the promise of God
And your own achieving.
There is no release from this,
There is only guidance and growth through it.

There are no new forms of temptation.
I have known them all,
Every one of them.

And the awful sense
Of a power still deeper,
At the very heart of you,
Perhaps near the heart of reality.

You may trust your Father.
He enabled me to overcome the world.
He will do the same for you.

Be released into joyful trust.

For thine
is the kingdom
and the power
and the glory,
for ever.
Amen.

You will need to add
Your own final word of praise.
It will rise up within you
Like a glad shout.

Affirming his final rule over all,
Knowing the ultimacy of his power,
Yielding deepest honor to him,

Pray then like this:

That he may truly rule your life,
That he may release in you his power,
That the wonder of his beauty may shine
Through the radiance of your being,
Now
And in the fullness of forever.

Amen.

III

A Contemporary Psalm

Bless the Lord, O my soul:
And all that is within me, bless his holy name.

i

Our need for knowledge,
Our love of beauty—
    The restless urge to create—
Let these bless the Lord.

Our delight in play,
Our wanting to laugh—
    The joy of being alive—
Let all these bless the Lord.

    Lest in playing games
        We lose the enjoyment of pleasure.
    Lest in singing songs
        We deaden the sound of delight.
    Lest in making things pretty
        We blur the vision of beauty.

With song and sound
With sense and word
With color and line
With motion and grace
Let us bless the Lord.

That the knowledge we gain
  May mirror the truth he is.
That the forms we shape
  May image the beauty he is.
That the songs we sing
  May voice the grace he gives.
That the games we play
  May reflect the joy he gives.

ii

Our striving for justice,
Our desire to live in harmony—
  The longing for peace—
Let these too bless the Lord.

For it is he who has set us in families
  That we may learn to love one another.
It is he who has drawn us together
  That we may share each other's strength.

Then why do we fail to love?
  Spoiling desire with shame.
  Making homes into nests of spite,
    Husbands and wives uncaring,
    Parents and children unloving.

Why do we abuse one another?
  One man taking his gain
    From the sweat of another man's face.
  Persons deprived of their rights
    Until they sink in sullen despair
    Or strike in angry rebellion.

Why do we live without trust?
  Nation poised against nation
    Each armed with inhuman might.
  Class guarded against class
    Each bent on its own private gain.

O Lord, how long?
Must it always be this way?
  Dare we hope for release
    From hatred and distrust?
  Shall we ever find escape
    Out of guarded, sullen fear?

iii

Let us have faith.
Let us dare hope.
  And with trust and honest faith,
  With love and true concern,
  With respect for every man,
  With regard for all mankind,
  Let us bless the Lord.

That the buildings we raise may be
   Shrines to our common good.
That the laws we write may be
   Charters of our shared humanity.
That the nations we build may be
   Forms for our broadening freedom.
That the homes we shape may be
   Shelters for nurturing love.

For it is in blessing the Lord
That we find our own blessedness.
   Knowing beauty to be his gift,
     We give grace to our lives.
   Knowing truth to be his will,
     We add wisdom to learning.
   Knowing love to be his way,
     We live at peace with one another.
   Knowing ourselves to be his creatures,
     We enter the fullness of our being.

Then bless the Lord, O my soul:
And all that is within me, bless his holy name.

ABOUT THE AUTHOR

Chester A. Pennington is professor of preaching and worship at The Iliff School of Theology, Denver, Colorado. For seventeen years he was minister of the Hennepin Avenue United Methodist Church, Minneapolis, Minnesota, and prior to that was a U.S. Navy chaplain (1943–45) and minister of various churches in New Jersey and New York.

Dr. Pennington is a graduate of Temple University, Drew University Theological Seminary, and Drew University (Ph.D.). He is the recipient of many awards and honors, including the Distinguished Service Award of the City of Minneapolis (1959), and is the author of numerous popular religious books, including *Liberated Love; Even So, Believe; With Good Reason; A More Excellent Way;* and *Half-Truths or Whole Gospel?;* and *Christian Counter Culture.*